turn your workload into work you love, is just one study away. Start now with this Field Manual!"

Brenda Haire, Integrator at Igniting Souls, Speaker, and Author of *Save the Butter Tubs!: Discover Your Worth in a Disposable World*

Praise for Sacred Work in Secular Places Field Manual Leader's Guide

"Work is hard for most people. But women seem to face a disproportionate share of situations that can steal our joy and make us wonder "what's the point?" This study provides real, authentic examples of what women experience at work and in life. You'll gain insight into how you can turn to God for guidance in even the most painful situations and be encouraged by what can happen when you follow His lead. The thought-provoking questions are sure to help you gain a more biblical perspective on your work. You'll see your work not only as a way to partner with God, but also as a way to love the people He has placed right there with you."

Catherine Gates, Senior Director of Content and Partnerships, WorkMatters.org

"If you have a heart to bring women together to deepen their walk with the Lord, this field manual is the perfect resource to help you make this prompting a reality. This small group leader's guide will give you a framework to build intimate community and facilitate transformational discussions. Joan Turley, Marian Ward and Teri

Capshaw bring you their collective wisdom and inspiration from their work and life experiences. Their authenticity and real-life stories will help you create a safe environment for women to break free from self-limiting beliefs, understand their worth, and propel them toward their potential. This step-by-step guide is all you need to be a catalyst for hope so needed by women today."

Linda Outka, Leadership Coach, Founder of Breakthrough Solutions, Inc. and author of *Pebbles in My Shoe: Three Steps to Breaking through Interpersonal Conflict*

"Whether you are a reluctant new leader or seasoned facilitator, this simple guide will help you create a space where women feel loved, accepted, and comfortable. You will see women blossom as they enjoy relationship-building fellowship while discovering their invaluable worth and work."

Niccie Kliegl, CEO Fulfill Your Legacy, and author of "The Legacy Series"

"This Field Manual will inspire and equip any woman with a heart for her co-workers and community. In it she will find both Scriptural truth and stories of the modern-day workplace demonstrating that God has a purpose for the labor of our hands. How we spend the waking hours of our day matters! This study is for any woman desiring to increase her influence and impact in the workplace so that she might be a force for love and a witness of God. Take these lessons to heart and see what God will do!"

Kimberly MacNeill, author/speaker, www.theinspirationlounge.org

"As I became an owner and partner in a business, I had the honor of meeting Joan and working through Sacred Work with her side by side. It showed me how we could promote, teach and believe in the ones who were entrusted to our care. Through hard times, this continuously pointed me to Jesus and reminded me WHO I work for, and WHY I was where I was.

I believe this Field Manual will do the same for you. Be lifted up, inspired and know you were made for this!"

Lauren Gish, Owner/Partner, Fruition Salon, fruition-salon.com

"I met Joan after owning a salon for 13 years. I was at a low point in my business and she kindly offered her consulting services as a gift. I agreed to meet with her because I felt the Lord was nudging me to do so even though I really just wanted to sell the salon or give it away.

Joan came in like a breath of fresh air and helped me remember why I wanted to be a salon owner and my purpose in having a business. Not only did she help me heal on the emotional side of being a business owner, but she helped me rebuild my business with the intentions God gave us before we opened the doors 17 years ago. She has helped us turn our business around and showed us how to grow. Her guidance and wisdom are invaluable.

I'm so excited Joan has created this incredible book. I pray *"Sacred Work in Secular Places Field Manual"* blesses you, your family and business in only the way Jesus can. Joan is a vessel sharing God's love for His people in the workplace."

Heather McCollum, Owner/Partner, Fruition Salon, fruitionsalon.com

"Don't believe the quote about doing what you love and you'll never work a day in your life. Work takes effort. You might love the work you do, but loving it doesn't mean it doesn't take effort. That is where this Field Manual comes in. It will help you navigate the work you do and see the bigger picture behind the daily grind. Work is sacred and learning how to

SACRED WORK IN SECULAR PLACES FIELD MANUAL

A Small Group Leader's Guide

JOAN L. TURLEY   MARIAN L. WARD   TERI CAPSHAW

CAPSHAW
MEDIA

Paperback ISBN: 978-1-951525-01-9
Ebook ISBN: 978-1-951525-01-9

Cover Design: Nathan Turley

Original Artwork: Valentina Migliore

Unless otherwise indicated, all Scripture quotations
are from the ESV® Bible (The Holy Bible, English
Standard Version®), copyright © 2001 by
Crossway, a publishing ministry of Good News
Publishers. Used by permission. All rights reserved.

Scripture taken from the New King James
Version®. Copyright © 1982 by Thomas Nelson.
Used by permission. All rights reserved.

Scripture quotations marked (NLT) are taken from

❀ Created with Vellum

Contents

An Open Letter to the Reluctant

Dear Small Group Leader,

I know how intimidating it can be to lead a group discussion! Don't worry, you are normal and you are enough!

Creating a space where women feel loved, accepted, and comfortable to be real is the goal here. There are no perfect groups and no perfect sessions, so let it happen and enjoy the relationship-deepening fellowship as you grow together.

These schedules are set up for a one-hour study, but I recommend a two-hour meeting, with the first hour centered around a meal or snacks and more casual interaction getting to know one another.

My small group organizes a little potluck for every session. I find the conversations while "breaking bread" together are some of the most valuable for relationship-building.

We see this principle modeled in the New Testament church:

> *"So continuing daily with one accord in the temple, and breaking bread from house to house, they ate their food with gladness and simplicity of heart, praising God and having favor with all the people." Acts 2:46-47a NKJV*

I'm not one for rules, but here are some guidelines to keep in mind:

1. Let it be messy. Like I said before, nothing here will be perfect! There are no perfect leaders, groups, or sessions.

2. Be yourself. This seems obvious, but can be difficult when you already feel vulnerable taking the bold step of starting a group. People will respond in ways you've never imagined when you've led by example in being real about your struggles and joys.

3. Don't be afraid of silence. When I was being trained as a college instructor, my mentor told me

to allow up to 12 seconds of silence after asking a question! It feels like forever, but it allows room for group members that might not otherwise speak up. (I rarely make it to 12 seconds before someone talks, so don't beat yourself up on this either).

4. Have fun. No really. This is vitally important for two reasons.

A) It strengthens bonds and you want a space where you can laugh together and also cry together.

B) Having fun is actually crucial to learning. It's how our brains are wired. Deeper learning accompanies emotion.

5. Know you are not alone. You are already equipped for this. In Ephesians 2:10, we are reminded of this. "For we are his workmanship created in Christ Jesus for good works, which God prepared beforehand that we might walk in them." (ESV)

If you have questions, please reach out! Shoot me an email at Marian@MarianLWard.com.

You were made to make a difference! I'm proud and excited for you. I'm praying for your continued courage as you take this huge step of faith!

Much love,

Marian L. Ward

How to Use This Book

The goal of the *Sacred Work in Secular Places Field Manual* is to fully equip you to reach the heart of what is most important without spending a lot of time planning.

Time segments that are given in each session agenda are merely suggestions to help you work within the timeframe. You will know your group better than anyone, so if the suggested time segments don't work, do what works for you.

These segments also will not usually add up to a full hour, so you have some cushion. It never hurts to have a discussion take longer...this is where the learning happens. It's especially great to add that cushion to your prayer time if available. Use the extra time as it best suits your group.

Here is a breakdown of each of the time segments included in each Bible study session:

Prayer/Welcome

This is your opportunity to get to know your group's needs. Try to be intentional to give all individuals a chance to share.

There is always a range of personalities and comfort levels with speaking out loud within a group. Some will never feel comfortable, but do your best to provide the time and space.

You may also have to balance that with gently tempering some of the more talkative members of your group.

Pray for your group members *by name*. It is important for them to hear you as the leader pray for them individually. Keep a notebook so you can write down their names and needs.

Content

These sections of text or video segments are drawn from three main sources: The Bible, *Made to Make a Difference*, and *Sacred Work in Secular Places*.

In most instances, Scripture is taken from the English Standard Version. Other versions are noted within the text.

Video content is available for purchase from our website: www.thennonnegotiables.com.

Sacred Work in Secular Places Field Manual: Participant's Guide and *Made to Make a Difference* are available for purchase on Amazon. *Sacred Work in Secular Places* is available wherever books are sold.

Discussion

This portion of the session is crucial to help learning become transformational for our lives through practical application and contributes to relationship-building for your group. After all, this is why we have Scripture as noted in II Timothy 3:16-17.

> All Scripture is inspired by God and is useful to teach us what is true and to make us realize what is wrong in our lives. It corrects us when we are wrong and teaches us to do what is right. God uses it to prepare and equip his people to do every good work. (NLT)

Don't be afraid of awkward silence. It can sometimes spur discussion. It's extremely difficult, but try to wait several seconds before starting to give your perspective. Count in your head if you have to.

It's very easy as a new and nervous leader to feel like you have to talk, but your group members need to have the opportunity to work through what they're learning in this way.

Debrief

In addition to opening the Scriptures and interpersonal fellowship, this is one of most important times during your session. The debrief is when you will "unpack" everything else. It will give you a quick assessment of your group's learning.

This is not a time to introduce any new content. The idea is to deepen understanding of the big takeaways of that particular session.

Do not worry about getting through each question. Often the best discussions simply need a nudge in the right direction.

Prayer/Closing

Just like the opening prayer time, the main objective is praying for and with your group members.

Most sessions provide a prompt for specific requests, but don't forget that you know and love your group better than anyone. Be confident that you know what's best and follow the guidance of the Holy Spirit.

Connect with Us

The back to the book includes information about the authors and an opportunity to connect with us.

We hope you thoroughly enjoy this study and we would love to connect directly with you via email and in our Facebook group.

To connect with us on Facebook, search @thenon-negotiables in your Facebook search bar to bring up our public page. Click on the "more" tab and select "groups." You can click to join our private group and we'll approve you as soon as possible.

Session One

MADE TO MAKE A DIFFERENCE

Welcome & Prayer (5 minutes)

Ask the Lord to open hearts and minds to His message as you begin this new study together.

Introductions (10-15 minutes)

Ask each group member to answer the following questions:

Tell us your name and what you do for work or ministry (including the work you do at home).

What do you hope to gain from our time together?

What do you hope to contribute to this group?

Content (5-10 minutes)

Play Session 1 Video 1 or read the "Woman's Worth" passage below aloud (from Made to Make a

Difference).

Woman's Worth

In light of the "me too" movement, it seems apparent and more critical than ever, that for the sake of all women, and especially for the sake of our daughters we reacquaint ourselves with the Creator's perspective on the true value and worth of woman—all the fiercely courageous, bold and beautiful things she brings to this world.

Yes! That is what we must do if we are to fully know God's original intent for woman. But here's the deal, we need a knowing that surpasses mere intellectual knowledge. We need a down-deep-in-our-bones kind of knowing, the kind of knowing that becomes such a part of our being that we cannot dissociate ourselves from it. Because to have that kind of knowing is to possess an unshakable confidence in the One in whose image we are created.

To gain that kind of knowing, we have to go back to the beginning, back to the garden—back to Genesis.

In Genesis 2:18 we read:

> Then the Lord God said, "It is not good for the man to be alone. I will make a helper who is just right for him." (NLT)

Sadly, as Alice Matthews writes, "Many Christians stumble over the word helper as the woman's work assignment. In our day, we use that word to describe someone like a plumber's apprentice, present to hand the plumber the right wrench at the right time. But that is far from the meaning of the Hebrew word used here."[1]

The Hebrew word in this text for woman [helper] is ezer k'negdo. And let me just say, the meaning behind these two words is far more precious than we could possibly imagine. More to the point, to discover what these words really mean is to understand the incredible value and worth of woman. God's glorious intent—the very purpose for which He created the woman—is profoundly noble and full of honor.

So, for that reason, we need to pause for a holy moment and appreciate the riches of the Scriptures. There's more than we realize to the familiar passages we read each day. Trust me, it does our feminine souls much good to soak in the water of His word.

Oh, I hope you can see how beautiful this is. An ezer k'negdo is not a lesser being, not an unequal being, and certainly not a postscript or an addendum.

Created in the image of God, she is an ezer k'negdo who reflects the glory of God in and through the vibrancy of her life as she collaborates with others and engages in matters of both home and business.

God holds woman in high regard. To be created as an ezer k'negdo is indeed a truly noble thing.

A simple but beautiful example is a story told about Mary Magdalene in the Gospel of John 20:11-18.

When Jesus appointed Mary Magdalene to go and tell the disciples that He was risen from the dead, He knew the societal constraints that had been placed upon women. He knew a woman's testimony was not considered credible. Yet, He commissioned her anyway. It was as though He was saying "Behold I make all things new. I have come to restore all that was lost in the fall, including the voice of woman."

And here's the good news: He is still calling ezer women to rise up and do brave things for His glory and for the benefit of all people.

It is our deepest desire that all women would come to know that they are deeply loved by God. Created to be ezer k'negdos, they are more than a post-script—they have been fearfully and beautifully made in the image of their maker.

Christ alone makes every woman worthy.

.   .   .

Discussion (10-15 minutes)

Have you ever heard this definition of "helper" or "helpmeet" before? What did you think of it?

How do you feel about thinking of yourself as an ezer k'negdo, "who reflects the glory of God in and through the vibrancy of her life"?

Had you ever considered this story about Mary Magdalene before? How does it make you feel to think that the risen Jesus showed himself to a woman first?

Why do you think you might feel less than worthy of this calling and empowerment of God?

Content (5-10 minutes)

Play Session 1 Video 2 or read the "Woman's Waiting" passage below aloud (from Made to Make a Difference).

Woman's Waiting

So, here's the deal: when it comes to coping with real life you can choose to "count it all joy" or you can let disappointment steal the joy from your life and leave a bitter taste in your mouth.

Sometimes it can feel like everything is going wrong, but what if God is as big as He says He is?

And what if you waste your life fighting against His plan because you can't see the bigger picture?

David Flood was a missionary who struggled with a problem like that. He and his wife, Svea, were missionaries in the Congo. In their first year they didn't make any progress—the most they seemed to accomplish was telling a little boy about Jesus. (He delivered food to their back door.) Svea was bedridden, sick with malaria, and pregnant.

After she gave birth to a baby girl, Aina, Svea died. Devastated and disappointed with God, David quit. He left the mission field—and left his baby daughter behind to be raised by other missionary couples.

As an adult Aina, now known as Aggie and married to an American pastor, received a Swedish religious magazine in the mail. It showed a grave with a cross bearing her birth mother's name.

She found someone to translate the article and discovered that the one little boy who gave his life to Jesus had spent a lifetime sharing the news in his village through a school he started. Even the village chief had converted to Christianity.

Aggie managed to go to Sweden, find her birth father, who had spent years drinking away his sorrows, and tell him that her mother hadn't died in vain.

Their work as missionaries had been successful after all.

He was overcome with emotion to realize that his time in the mission field wasn't wasted. God had been working the entire time.

Finally, free from bitterness, David reconciled with his God and his daughter.

Years later Aggie and her husband attended a conference in London where the Superintendent of the national church of Zaire—representing about 110,000 believers—was speaking.

After his presentation she went up and introduced herself to him. That moment is captured in her biography:

> *"Aggie could not help going up afterward to ask him if he had ever heard of David and Svea Flood. "I am their daughter." The man began to weep. "Yes, madam," the man replied in French, his words then being translated into English.*
>
> *"It was Svea Flood who led me to Jesus Christ. I was the boy who brought food to your parents before you were born. In fact, to this day your mother's grave and her memory are honored by all of us."*

He embraced her in a long, sobbing hug. Then he continued, "You must come to Africa to see, because your mother is the most famous person in our history."[2]

In time, that is exactly what Aggie Hurst and her husband did. They were welcomed by cheering throngs of villagers.

She even met the man who so many years before, when she was less than a month old, had been hired by her father to carry her down the mountain in a soft bark hammock.

DISCUSSION (10-15 MINUTES)

What if you believed God was as big as He says He is? What would you do differently if you fully believed that without any fear?

What stood out to you about Aggie's story? Why?

What does her story tell us about the power of saying yes to God, even when the task seems meaningless?

DEBRIEF (20 MINUTES)

(This is where we unpack the whole evening.)

What are some things we talked about that really stood out to you? What about it was significant to you?

How would you explain the important points we covered to someone who wasn't here?

What is something we talked about that you've never thought about before?

If you only had one big takeaway from our discussion, what would it be?

Study Overview

Here you can share what participants can expect in the coming week.

In the next few sessions we will be going over the content in *Sacred Work in Secular Places*—a book written to help Christians fall in love with their work and discover the incredible impact they can have every day in every role.

For the deepest experience you can read each section of the book over the course of this Bible study.

Each of the next four sessions will be dedicated to a section of the book:

Session 2 "Why I Hated Work: The Not Enoughs Must Die!"

Session 3 "Why God Loves Work: A Biblical, Historical, and Contemporary View of 'Work'"

Session 4 "Why You Can Love Work: Becoming a Difference-Maker"

Session 5 "Work Strategy: There Will be Battles: But God Will Win"

Session six, the final session of our study, will bring everything together with a look at how we can all find a seat at the table in life.

Closing & Prayer

Ask how you can pray for each woman as you journey together for the next several weeks.

_____

_____

_____

_____

_____

_____

_____

_____

_____

_____

_____

Session Two

YOU ARE ENOUGH!

Welcome & Prayer (5 minutes)
Ask the Lord to open hearts and minds to His message and that each woman in the room will internalize that, in Christ, she is enough.

Content (5-10 minutes)
Play Session 2 Video 1 or read the "God at Work" passage below aloud (from pp. 13-14, 32 of Sacred Work in Secular Places).

GOD AT WORK

The simple of act of remembering that God was faithful, even in the dark where I could not see His hand, caused a shift in my thinking and praying. I knew intuitively that somehow, someway, change was coming: kind of like the scene in Mary Poppins when Bert pauses mid-sentence, looks around, notices the wind is changing, and begins to sing, "Winds in the east, mist coming in, like somethin' is brewin' and 'bout to begin. Can't put me finger on what lies in store, but I fear what's to happen all happened before."[1]

Just like Bert knew that something marvelous was astir, I too knew that God was up to something. And, just as quick as Mary Poppins blew in from the east, God began to show up at my work in amazing little ways, proving to me that my lack of a degree did not matter to Him one tiny bit! I might have been a nobody to everyone else, but to God I was a somebody—I was His beloved child. He could and would move mountains on my behalf.

When I say I was a nobody, I mean I really was a nobody! During my time working for the school district, one of my jobs was to answer the phones. My day consisted of repeating the words, "Hello, thank you for calling XYZ Junior High. This is Joan, how may I help you?"

I was just the lady who answered phones, nothing more. I wasn't even in with the in-crowd of the paraprofessionals. When they went to lunch, I was not invited. I don't know why, but they never included me (and yes, it hurt). I was at the bottom rung and had no clout with anyone . . . except for one school counselor, Laurie. She was well-respected by the higher-ups and deeply loved by the student body.

She just loved people, and she loved me. More importantly, she saw the gifts that God had given to me when no one else did, and then when the time was right, she drew attention to them.

One day all of the counselors were out of the building, attending a work-mandated training seminar, when both parents of one of our students were killed in a horrible accident. When the students learned this, a profound sadness swept across the school.

As soon as the news reached Laurie, who was the lead counselor, she called the principal of the school and urged him, "Put somebody at the front desk to answer phones, and get Joan in that counseling office! For over a decade, she worked in a full-time ministry bringing hope to the brokenhearted. She is well-equipped to listen and extend compassion to our kids."

And, just like that, I was accompanied to the counseling office to comfort the students as they mourned that tragic event. In a building filled with highly-educated staff, God in His sovereignty chose to use an uneducated, degreeless paraprofessional to bring hope and healing.

A heart to serve, to pour into the lives of others, and to add value wherever you can will trump lack of education every time. A serving heart needs no credentials. It sees a need and says, "How can I help?" In the years ahead, I would be called upon to mediate disagreements between students and between teachers and to speak to the entire teaching staff on the value of mentoring. Although I was still an uneducated paraprofessional, in serving others and meeting their needs I began to experience that God was in the business of moving through people, regardless of their level of education.

Now, don't get me wrong, I love education. Both of my children have earned college degrees, and I am only a few courses short of an associate's degree. The lesson to be learned, though, is this: God is in the business of partnering with us right where we are. He is never limited by the Not Enoughs in our lives. All that He requires is a heart to serve people.

Armed with the knowledge that God has a divine platform for your life, shall we take a look at God's ultimate purpose for the work of our hands?

Read on, beloved, and you will discover that work was meant to be a blessing and not a curse. Whatever roadblocks you've encountered, kick them to the curb, send them back to the hell-hole from which they came, and go run your race. You were meant to shine for God's glory in the platform of His choosing.

So, what about you? What Not Enough lies have you believed? God delights in you just as you are, and He is not limited by your Not Enoughs.

DISCUSSION (20 MINUTES)

What are some areas where you do not feel like enough?

What parts of Joan's story resonated the most with you? Why?

Think about a time someone gave something to you that they might've seen as simple and insignificant, but made an impact on you.

What did they say or do? What was the impact?

Why do you think that has stayed with you?

Content (5-10 minutes)

Play Session 2 Video 2 or read the "The Widow of Zarephath" passage below aloud (from I Kings 17:8-16 ESV).

The Widow of Zarephath

8 Then the word of the LORD came to him, 9 "Arise, go to Zarephath, which belongs to Sidon, and dwell there. Behold, I have

commanded a widow there to feed you." 10 So he arose and went to Zarephath. And when he came to the gate of the city, behold, a widow was there gathering sticks. And he called to her and said, "Bring me a little water in a vessel, that I may drink." 11 And as she was going to bring it, he called to her and said, "Bring me a morsel of bread in your hand." 12 And she said, "As the LORD your God lives, I have nothing baked, only a handful of flour in a jar and a little oil in a jug. And now I am gathering a couple of sticks that I may go in and prepare it for myself and my son, that we may eat it and die." 13 And Elijah said to her, "Do not fear; go and do as you have said. But first make me a little cake of it and bring it to me, and afterward make something for yourself and your son. 14 For thus says the LORD, the God of Israel, 'The jar of flour shall not be spent, and the jug of oil shall not be empty, until the day that the LORD sends rain upon the earth.'" 15 And she went and did as Elijah said. And she and he and her household ate for many days. 16 The jar of flour was not spent, neither did the jug of oil become empty, according to the word of the LORD that he spoke by Elijah.

Discussion (20 minutes)

Think about this widow's story. What's in your hand?

What do you think might hold you back from sharing what's in your hand?

Debrief (10-15 minutes)

This is our opportunity to review and process takeaways.

What are some of the things we talked about this evening?

How did it feel to share some of your not enoughs?

How did it feel to reflect on a time when someone made an impact on you?

What are some ways even this week you could share what's in your hand?

What is something we talked about that you'd never thought about before?

What is something we talked about that you could use as soon as you leave here?

Closing & Prayer

Pray that the Lord will help each woman see the worth of what is in her hand this week.

_____

_____

_____

_____

_____

_____

_____

_____

_____

_____

_____

_____

_____

_____

_____

_____

_____

Session Three

GOD'S INVITATION TO PARTNER WITH HIM

Welcome & Prayer (5 minutes)

Take a few minutes to welcome each person and pray their hearts are prepared for this session's message.

CONTENT (5-10 MINUTES)

Play Session 3 Video 1 or read the "Created for Good Works" passage below aloud (from pp. 40-43 of Sacred Work in Secular Places).

Created for Good Works

Knowing that God has called me by name and has invited me into a partnership with Him has had a profound impact upon my life: so much so, that it has kept me going even in my darkest days.

In 2009, I lost my twenty-two-month old nephew to tickborne meningitis. It was a senseless and preventable death, which made it all the more horrendous. I have never experienced such intense sorrow and pain.

The loss of a child is overwhelming. I loved that precious little boy with every ounce of my being. I was holding his mama's hand when she brought him into the world, I heard his first cry, and I cut his umbilical cord. It was love at first sight. To lose that child was devastating to our family. That little boy's death remains the most significant loss I have ever encountered . . . there is an ache in our hearts that will not go away.

When I returned to the solitude of my home after burying that precious child, I did not want to go back to work. I did not want to engage the world on any level. When we lost that boy, our world stopped while everyone else kept moving on. I know, life goes on, but it seemed so unfair. How could I be expected to walk into a place where people were laughing and smiling while my heart was breaking into a million pieces?

On the morning I was scheduled to go back to work, I sat with a cup of coffee in my hand and a Bible on my lap, covered in a cloak of sorrow. I can tell you I did not want to drag myself into the workplace. I did not want to talk to anyone, let alone see anyone's happy face.

But in those early morning hours, before the crack of dawn, still and quiet, I began to sense God speaking: Oh, Joan, don't you remember? I pre-ordained good works for your hands to do, and if you stay here wrapped in grief, you will miss the good things I have arranged for you. Work, my child, is blessing, not a curse. Don't sit out and miss all I have for you—get up, my child, and go to work!

That little word of encouragement, "work is a blessing, not a curse," reminded me that there were blessings to be enjoyed—blessings that had been prepared for me in advance of this great sorrow. In the quietness of that moment, God reminded me that He knew the weight of my sorrow.

He too had lost a Son, His One and Only. He also knew that in putting my hand to the plow, joy would come again. Ephesians 2:10 says,

> "For we are God's workmanship, created in Christ Jesus to do good works, which God prepared in advance for us to do" (NIV).

As I pondered that God had prepared good work for me in advance of every heartbreak I would ever encounter, I remembered a message that my pastor, Gregg Matte, had once preached, called "More

Than a Paycheck." His text was Colossians 3:22-24 and Thessalonians 4:12. That message was life-changing for me.

It was the moment I finally understood once and for all, that my work, secular though it may be, was absolutely holy to God. And not only was it holy, it was a place hand-picked by God for me to shine for His glory. That day, I fell head over heels in love with the work of my hands, because I knew I was right where God wanted me.

I would love to share a little bit of Gregg's wisdom with you, with the hope that you too will know once and for all that your place of work is one of the greatest platforms you will ever have for impacting the lives of those who have been placed within your sphere of influence.

Let's begin with a review of the passages Gregg cited:

> "Let every employee listen well and follow the instructions of their employer, not just when their employers are watching, and not in pretense, but faithful in all things. For we are to live our lives with pure hearts in the constant awe and wonder of our Lord God. Put your heart and soul into every activity you do, as though you are doing it for the Lord himself and not merely for others."

Colossians 3:22-23 (The Passion Translation)

". . . Work with your own hands . . . so *that your daily life may win respect of outsiders* and so that you will not be dependent on anybody." I Thessalonians 4:11-12 (NIV, emphasis mine)

As you look at each of these verses, can you not hear the underlying message? Work is for an impact, not just an income! Your job is the channel for impact. Gregg asked us to consider the following:

"Does it seem right that Jesus would die on a cross, Moses would wander through the desert, Paul would be martyred for the faith, Peter would be crucified upside down, and others would be slain with swords, so that today...you and I would acquire leather interiors? Does this seem odd? Or does it seem more right that all the above happened so that you and I could come into our work place *not just to have an income but to make an impact?*" [1]

God loves work! In listening to Gregg's teaching, I finally made the connection that God, who ordains our steps, sovereignly places us in specific work surroundings. He chooses our platform and He places us where He needs a light that will shine "in all of life, in every sphere—for the glory of God and in obedience to His Word."[2]

Gregg challenged us to consider that whatever our title or position may be, it's just a cover to usher in His love, that hearts may be mended in a broken world. From that day forward I saw myself as a Christian, disguised as a Director of Operations, with a mandate from God to serve those beautiful people He had placed within my sphere of influence.

The pages of Scripture consistently reveal there is no separation between the sacred and the secular! His Word speaks not only of priests, prophets, and apostles, but of shepherds, potters, perfumers, bricklayers, educators, physicians, fishermen—the list goes on and on—who were all called to live in faithful response to God's call upon their lives.

Look at 1 Corinthians 7:17. It says, "And don't be wishing you were someplace else or with someone else. Where you are right now is God's place for you. Live and obey and love and believe right there..." (MSG)

Timothy Keller says that in this passage, "Paul is not referring . . . to church ministries, but to common social and economic tasks—'secular jobs,' we might say—and naming them God's callings and assignments." He continues, "the implication is clear: Just as God equips Christians for building up the Body of Christ, so he equips all people with talents and gifts for various kinds of work, for the purpose of building up the human community."[3]

Oh, I hope you get it, and I hope it sets your heart on fire. Your work matters. Your light is *needed* in this dark world.

DISCUSSION (15 MINUTES)

Consider some of the verses in this week's session. How does it make you feel to think that you are already equipped to do good work(s)?

What is something you would do if you really believed God had already empowered you to do it?

If you don't go to a "job", how might this discussion relate to your ministry work? Your work in the home?

What do you think it means to "not just have an income, but an impact"?

CONTENT (5-10 MINUTES)

Play Session 3 Video 2 or read the "Time for Action" passage below aloud (from pp. 51-53 of Sacred Work in Secular Places).

A Time for Action

We're living in world that no longer believes in absolute truth. However, even though we live in a world where truth no longer matters and Christianity is seen as narrow and intolerant, we still have opportunities. Regardless of its worldview, every human heart remains the same—in need of healing and deep compassion.

God has established work as a means of connection with those who need His grace and mercy. This is not the time to shrink back from seeming "too Christian." This is the time to live out the gospel!

I think this could be our finest hour. With truth being challenged and Christianity called into question, the postmodern era bears a striking resemblance to the days of the early church.

Indeed, they were difficult days for Christians, yet because the love of God was so outstandingly demonstrated through the lives of the early saints, the message of God and His love for mankind flourished in that hostile world. Like the early saints, it is of utmost importance that our actions speak louder than our words.

In his book, *Every Good Endeavor*, Timothy Keller shares the story of a woman who made a big mistake at her new job—a mistake that could have gotten her fired. But instead, her boss went to his superior and took responsibility for her mistake. In doing so, he lost some of his reputation and good standing. The woman couldn't understand why her boss would take the blame for her! She kept asking him why, why would he do that for her?

Finally, he relented and told her,

"I am a Christian. That means among other things that God accepts me because Jesus Christ took the blame for things that I have done wrong. He did that on the cross. That is why I have the desire and sometimes the ability to take the blame for others."[4] In response, the woman simply asked him where he went to church! The Christ-like selflessness of her boss was a transformative force in this woman's life.

While it may not be as culturally acceptable to openly share the Gospel, nothing can prevent us from living it. When we allow the gospel to shape our character and our actions toward others, the world takes notice and is attracted to the Gospel.

We are given a huge opportunity to make a difference in the workplace when we choose to "respect and treat those who believe differently as valued equals in the workplace and at the same time . . . be unashamed to be identified with Jesus."[5]

In this postmodern world our actions matter: not just in how we treat our co-workers, but also in the quality of our work. "As we do good work that reflects God's character graciously, purely, morally, ethically, creatively, and excellently, we unleash His beauty. People see God."[6]

Our work is the greatest platform we have to express God's desire to mend the wounded hearts of His beloved children. So do good work and get noticed—not for your sake, but that your circle of influence might grow for the blessing of many! We are called to serve that others might come to know the Love that has transformed our lives.

Here's the deal: your workplace is filled with people who are brokenhearted. Find a way to connect and show some love! I fell in love with work when I fell in love with the people, plain and simple. In today's postmodern world our workplaces are a wonderful melting pot of every culture and race. If we see our work as a place to love others, I promise you, beautiful things will happen.

Just start looking for creative ways to show others they are of immeasurable worth, simply because they are made in the image of God.

I will never forget the time that a friend of mine at work, Adiva, shared with me that her sister was going through a painful divorce and was moving back to be near my friend and her extended family. Her sister was a precious single mom, raising two adorable little boys, and the three of them had endured great rejection and loss of love. It was a painful time for her sister and the whole family.

I asked Adiva if we could throw a housewarming party for her sister. She tilted her head and gave me a blank look. "What's a housewarming party?" she asked. You see, Adiva was from a completely different culture and religion and had never heard of the concept! I explained what it was, and that I believed if we could gather a group of women together for the purpose of loving and encouraging her sister's heart, it just might lighten her load just a bit.

So, we did it! An unlikely, diverse group of Christian, Jewish, and Muslim women gathered in that room, and we laughed, cried, and prayed for a bright new future for Adiva's sister. That is how loving your neighbor as yourself is done!

Discussion (10 minutes)

What are some ways to share the Gospel that don't necessarily need words?

Think about Joan's story of throwing a party for her coworker. What is something you could do to serve others that might be as simple as a housewarming party?

. . .

DEBRIEF (15 MINUTES)

What is something we discussed that you hadn't thought about before?

What part of the discussion stood out with you the most today? Why?

Have you ever experienced someone showing you grace in an unexpected situation? What did that look like?

How might you join the sacred and the secular in your life as soon as you leave here?

CLOSING & Prayer

_____

_____

_____

_____

_____

_____

_____

_____

Session Four

THERE IS ROOM FOR YOU!

Welcome & Prayer (5 minutes)

Take a few minutes to welcome each person and pray their hearts are prepared for this session's message.

CONTENT (5-10 MINUTES)

Play Session 4 Video 1 or read the "Room Enough for Me" passage below aloud (from Genesis 26:17-22 ESV and pp. 55-56 of Sacred Work in Secular Places).

> 17 So Isaac departed from there and encamped in the Valley of Gerar and settled there. 18 And Isaac dug again the wells of water that had been dug in the days of

Abraham his father, which the Philistines had stopped after the death of Abraham. And he gave them the names that his father had given them. 19 But when Isaac's servants dug in the valley and found there a well of spring water, 20 the herdsmen of Gerar quarreled with Isaac's herdsmen, saying, "The water is ours." So he called the name of the well Esek, because they contended with him. 21 Then they dug another well, and they quarreled over that also, so he called its name Sitnah. 22 And he moved from there and dug another well, and they did not quarrel over it. So he called its name Rehoboth, saying, "For now the LORD has made room for us, and we shall be fruitful in the land."

There was a man named Isaac who dug a well. After he finished, some neighboring herdsmen came and claimed it as their own. Rather than quarrel and stir up strife, Isaac moved on and dug another well. (Been there, done that, I thought. That reminded me of my experience with a colleague.) Again, more herdsmen came and claimed this well too. (Hmm, that reminded me of all the professionals at the nonprofit who quickly outshone me and made my work redundant. This story was hitting close to home.) So, Isaac moved on and built a third well. This time, no one came to steal the work of his hands! Isaac called the well Rehoboth, which means "room enough for me" (Gen 26:19-22 ESV).

Oh my gosh. That was exactly what I been praying for—a place where there would be room enough for me. That word, Rehoboth, became an anchor for my soul. I began to pray over and over, "God, if I must work, please bring me to that place where there is room enough for me. Bring me to a place where my gifts will shine for your glory. Would you bring me to Rehoboth?"

Within weeks of stumbling upon that story of Isaac and his wells, God intervened in the middle of my brokenness and led me to a place where there was finally room enough for me. As I was praying for Rehoboth, my boss, Katherine, was praying for me too. She prayed that God would bring me to a "safe place." In fact, she approached her friend, the CEO of a salon and spa, and asked if she had a position open for me.

In February 2006, I was hired as Client Appointment Coordinator. And oh, yes—the Not Enough Leadership roadblock was smashed to smithereens as I flourished in my Rehoboth. I walked into my destiny; the sweet spot God had been preparing for me all those years ago when I first met Him in the morning at my cozy kitchen table.

There is a Rehoboth for every child of God. I do not know how many wells you may have to dig, but don't quarrel when someone steals your well. Move on, dear child, and dig another, knowing that the next one you dig could be your Rehoboth.

This book has been written for all of you that desperately long for your own Rehoboth.

Life is hard, and we never fully arrive this side of heaven; but we do get glimpses of His magnificent hand divinely placed upon our lives. As we share those moments in our lives with one another, when suddenly the clouds part and we see His plan . . . that is when we encourage one another to stay the course and rediscover that we, like the saints of old, have been called by a Most Holy God. I offer you my simple stories, stories of an ordinary working woman, who has discovered that work is more than a paycheck; it's an amazing platform for His glory. It's a partnership with God.

DISCUSSION (15 MINUTES)

Consider this concept of "Rehoboth." How would you respond and reach out to others if you truly believed there was "room enough" for you?

If you believe God has a specific calling for you, what is it and how did you discover it?

If you don't believe that, why not?

· · ·

Play Session 4 Video 2 or read the "Chewed Up and Spit Out" passage below from pp. 59-61 of Sacred Work in Secular Places).

Chewed Up and Spit Out

I could see the anger on her face as she came charging towards the counter I stood behind. What in the world could have made Kim so mad? At that moment, I was really thankful for the counter between us, but no physical barrier could protect me from her verbal onslaught. She was loud, she was rude and obnoxious to say the least, and everybody within earshot knew that I was getting the full force of Kim's anger. Someone had made a mistake in booking Kim's appointments, and someone was going to pay for it.

Wave after wave, she ripped me to shreds in front of co-workers and clients. Warm tears rose in my eyes and I tried to blink them back. Everyone was looking at me. I stood there completely humiliated. In all my years in the workforce I had never seen such unprofessionalism. Never had I been the punching bag of a co-worker's tyrannical behavior. But then again, I had pretty much worked in safe places—this was Babylon, and these were her people.

It was surreal; it seemed like everything moved in slow motion as I looked around to observe the shock on people's faces. She had made a fool of herself, but that didn't comfort me at all. How I found my voice, I will never know. With little more than I whisper I simply said, "Excuse me," walked away to a private corner, and fell apart.

Alone and feeling sorry for myself, I let the tears flow freely. As I tried to calm myself down and get a handle on what had just happen, I seemed to hear God say, Go serve Kim. I was outraged. I couldn't believe that God would actually ask me to go serve that woman who had just been so mean to me. I looked up at the ceiling as though I was staring into the face of God. "God, did you not see what just happened?" I said. "Didn't you see how she treated me? She just chewed me up and spit me out in front of everyone. I am not the one who should be serving her; that woman owes me an apology." And He seemed to say, Oh, Joan, there is a bigger picture here. This is not about you. Trust me child, and please go serve Kim.

I would like to say that I followed God's prompting with a cheerful heart, but I was not the least bit enthusiastic about His directive. Exasperated, I marched off to the kitchen and grabbed an ice-cold glass out of the freezer. I wrapped it with a white paper napkin, filled it with ice cubes and fresh water and placed a slice of lemon on the rim. It looked beautiful, like something that would be served at an elegant restaurant. (I was so mad and hurt at the time that I'm glad it didn't cross my mind to spit in it until much later).

I walked to her station and quietly said, "Here Kim, I thought you might like a glass of ice-cold water. I know how hard you work. You're on your feet all day long, and I appreciate everything that you do." She looked at me eyes wide, mouth open. It must have been difficult to fathom that the woman she'd just kicked like an old dog was standing in front of her with a gift in hand. I could see the shame on her face. She was visibly shaken. I set the glass down and quietly walked away.

At the end of the day, I saw her slowly shuffling towards the exit door, her head hung low. It looked as if she carried the weight of the world upon her shoulders. By the grace of God and that alone, I walked over to her, put my arm around her shoulder, and softly said, "Oh Kim, I'm so sorry for that mix-up we had earlier today." She looked at me with the saddest of eyes and somberly replied, "I'm sorry, too."

DISCUSSION (15 MINUTES)

Have you ever felt like Joan in this story? How did you respond?

How would it have been different if you chose to serve in that moment?

What are some (creative, new) ways to show others they are of immeasurable worth?

What do you think it means to open your heart to others?

Debrief (10 minutes)

What is something we discussed that you hadn't thought about before?

How might you be able to open your "home" to those you work with? (off-campus hospitality)

What are opportunities presented in our present culture that might not have been available in the past? For women specifically? For connections with nonbelievers?

If you were to tell someone else what the one takeaway was from this session, what would you say?

What is one small thing you can do tomorrow to show someone they are of immeasurable worth?

Closing & Prayer

Ask the Lord to protect them and help them as they step out in faith to minister to others in new ways this week.

_____

_____

_____

_____

_____

_____

_____

_____

_____

_____

_____

_____

_____

_____

_____

_____

Session Five

YOU ARE EQUIPPED!

Welcome & Prayer (5 minutes)

Take a few minutes to welcome each person and pray that they will be lovingly challenged through this session.

CONTENT (5-10 MINUTES)

Play Session 5 Video 1 or read the "The Girl in the Pink Shirt" and "A&B Relationships" passage below aloud (from pp. 83-88 of Sacred Work in Secular Places).

The Girl in the Pink Shirt

I was sitting behind a mountain of paperwork stacked high upon my desk when I first saw the beautiful girl in the hot pink shirt. I glanced over the rim of my bifocals and noted her hourglass figure, gorgeous hair, and impeccable dress. She was a picture of femininity and grace. She had come to interview for an entry-level position. Though she looked a little nervous, she displayed an easy smile that seemed to speak of warmth and friendliness.

Her resume was very impressive. However, prior to the interview, our management team had asked why she applied for an entry-level position when, according to her resume, she was overqualified. That should have been a huge red flag, and we should have explored it thoroughly, but we didn't. We were under intense pressure to replace a high-performing stylist who had abruptly resigned, so we ignored our intuition.

The woman interviewed fantastically! She was charming, witty, and charismatic. She offered everything we were looking for, and then some! Carried away with her magnetic personality (and extremely embellished resume), we hired her on the spot. Not only did we hire her, we immediately pro-moted her to our elite team of stylists.

Had we insisted that she earn the right to be in-cluded on our team of highly educated profession-als, as had been required of every member on that team, we would have discovered that she had rightly applied for an entry-level position. That gal had a lot to learn, including how to treat her peers.

Nonetheless, with high hopes, we welcomed the charismatic, gorgeous lady in the hot pink shirt to our team of the most sought-after stylists in Houston.

It took less than a few weeks to recognize that we were in for a bumpy ride. She was lacking in many skills. She knew it and so did everyone else, but "teamwork" was not part of her vocabulary. Rather than endear herself to her teammates and humbly ask for help, she strutted about the place as if everyone was beneath her. It was awful. She cunningly pointed her finger at others, whispered behind everyone's back, and stirred the pot wherever she could. She treated her peers with sharp contempt and alienated herself from just about everybody.

Our Judas made enemies quicker than she could make friends. She was miserable, and she was hellbent on making others miserable, too. The team was on pins and needles, and many were often in tears. She got on everyone's last nerve. I regretted the day we hired her. I hated what was happening . . . especially in my own heart. I couldn't recall a time I had ever harbored such feelings of resentment for anyone.

Even though I smiled at her outwardly, inwardly I was full of anger and fury. She had brought dissension and disharmony into the salon, and I just wanted her to go away! I kept remembering the young woman we had interviewed—that charismatic, good-looking gal—and I couldn't help but wonder, *what went wrong?*

Then it hit me—we'd hired a Judas, a betrayer in our midst. I didn't know what to do. The thought of betrayal and the destruction that follows made me sick to my stomach. I thought about Jesus and wondered how He put up with His Judas, let alone love the man who would hand him over for crucifixion?

In that moment, I wasn't one bit like Jesus. I had no love in my heart for this young woman. Moreover, I did not want to be crucified. Yet, I had a feeling that was exactly what was going to happen.

A&B Relationships

In the midst of that terrible season, I was attending a marriage and family counseling class at The College of Biblical Studies. One night, during a class discussion, my dam of self-control burst.

I shared with the class what I was dealing with, and then, in unbridled fury, all of my pent-up frustration spewed out like vomit. I blurted out, "Honestly, I think I hate this girl! She's making my life a living hell. She's the most un-teachable person I have ever known, she is a Judas in my midst and I will *not* be crucified by this twit of a woman!"

I was horrified at the intensity of my anger. At that moment there was zero evidence of the love of God residing inside of me. I was so ashamed.

Thank God for divine intervention and for a wise course instructor who looked beyond my rage to see the pain in my heart. I had taken a hit on the battlefield of life, and I needed someone to carry me off the battlefield into the safety of my Father's love.

Without a word of accusation or condemnation, my course instructor, Jacobi Lewis, walked to the whiteboard. He picked up the blue maker and drew a large capital A and a capital B on the board. All eyes were on Mr. Lewis when he turned to face me. He looked right at me and said, "Joan, I think I can help you."

Mr. Lewis asked me, "Do you believe God is sovereign?" I sulkily replied, "Yes, I believe God is sovereign."

Then he said, "Well, if God is sovereign, then everyone who enters your life has been placed there by His hand. No one comes into your life by accident."

He pointed to the capital A and B on the board and said, "Therefore, you will either be in an A or a B relationship with every person who enters your life. The letter B stands for Builder. Let me ask you this: who can you build?"

I responded, "Well, I can only build those who want to be built—those who are teachable."

He responded, "Exactly!"

He went on to explain, "If you cannot be in a Builder relationship with someone, then your only option is an A relationship. In fact, if a B relationship is impossible, the only reason God sent her into your life was for an A relationship."

So, I asked the inevitable question: "What does A stand for?"

Looking me square in the eyes, he said, "A stands for Ambassador of Love."

He paused to let that thought sink in deeply, then proceeded, "This person who has caused you so much pain, God never intended you to fix. Right now, she's broken and unteachable. Don't even try to fix her—you can't! She was sent to you for one reason, and one reason only: that you might be an Ambassador of Love to her. Stop trying to build her; that's not why she's in your life."

Those words changed everything, and the tears fell like raindrops.

I wept for the beautiful girl in the hot pink shirt, and I wept with a heart full of gratitude for this fresh understanding. The anger, bitterness and frustration that had consumed me for months vanished instantly.

I knew what I had to do. I needed to ask for her forgiveness.

As she entered the salon, when she walked past my desk, I reached out my hand and said, "Hey, I need to talk with you, could you sit down for just a minute?" I smiled at her and gestured to the empty chair beside my desk. I could tell she was skeptical and unsure, but reluctantly she sat down.

Quietly I said, "I need to ask your forgiveness. I have not given you the benefit of the doubt, nor have I taken the time to genuinely listen when you asked to be heard. For that, I am sorry. Please know that this empty chair is for you, too. From now on, I promise that I will make time to listen. Will you please forgive me?"

I could see the shock and disbelief on her face, but I could also see relief. I continued, "I know there's been a wall between us, and that's on me, not you. I just want you to know, you are always welcome to this empty chair, and I will hear you out. I am sorry."

She said, "I forgive you," and then we chatted about small stuff and shared a laugh or two, anything to move us forward and put the past behind us.

When I let go of the Builder responsibility and embraced the Ambassador opportunity, everything changed in our relationship. I was free to love, not to fix, and she was freed to just be herself: a person in need of a little kindness and love.

It was amazing how quickly the atmosphere shifted within the entire salon. It was especially delightful when a bouquet of hot pink flowers was hand-delivered to my desk by the girl in the hot pink shirt.

There will be people in our lives who we cannot build. It doesn't matter why. What matters is that we recognize whether to spend our efforts building or simply loving. Spend your energy on those you can build, and spend your love on those you can't.

Those who just need love will probably only be in your life for a short season. They will move on to other pastures, but they will always remember the love that impacted their lives for that one brief season.

Discussion (10 minutes)

Have you ever dealt with the "girl in the hot pink shirt"? How did you respond to that person?

Would you have done something similar to Joan? If not, what would you do differently?

How would you explain, in your own words, the concept of A & B Relationships?

How might this concept help you think about your relationships differently?

CONTENT (5-10 MINUTES)

Play Session 5 Video 2 or read the "Blindsided and Dumbfounded" passage below aloud (from pp. 90-96 of Sacred Work in Secular Places).

Blindsided and Dumbfounded

I was looking for a way to connect with Liam. He was our new hire, and I hadn't yet invested in some quality one-on-one time with him. I had an errand to run for the company, so, I asked him to come along. I thought it would be the perfect opportunity for small talk and the beginning of a meaningful work-related relationship. I couldn't have been more wrong. It was the most perplexing discussion I'd ever had, with consequences I never imagined.

I remember almost every word of our conversation. In my mind, I can still see us driving around the streets of Houston on that hot summer day when he launched into a diatribe about the Christians he had known.

He did not like Christians, and the cynicism in his voice lead me to believe that he had experienced a good deal of hurt from the believers he had encountered. It made me sad. I, too, had often been hurt over the way some believers treated gay people. It made my heart sick.

I nodded my head, and continued to listen as he ranted and raged against Christianity in general. My goodness, what was this guy gonna do when he found out his new boss was a Christian? Would he believe I was sorry he'd had such bad experiences with Christians, and that I understood where he was coming from?

I got his anger, I really did. For a long time, I didn't know how to hold on to my Biblical convictions and still embrace those who were opposed to them.

But Liam did not personally know me, nor did he have any knowledge of my deeply-held belief. He had no way of knowing that he would be respected and appreciated, regardless of his sexuality or his robust opinions about Christians. The more he talked, the more I knew I needed to let him know that I was a Christian—and, moreover, that I understood why he felt the way he did.

So, when he slowed down long enough to catch his breath and let me get a word in edgewise, I simply said, "Liam, I am so sorry that has been your experience with other Christians. It makes me really sad because I'm a Christian."

I continued, "I have many friends who don't share my beliefs. Some are straight, and some are gay. Some are black, and some are white. Some are Democrat, and some are Republican. We don't always see eye to eye, yet we are thick as thieves and friends indeed.

Liam, I can tell you this: come life or even death, no matter what my friends and I may face, we are friends first and we will stand together. In their darkest hours, regardless of our differences, they can count on me."

I think he was genuinely shocked to discover that I was a Christian, because he didn't say much after that and he kept the conversation really light. I honestly thought he grasped I was offering an olive branch, and that I was openly sorry that he had had such repulsive experiences with other Christians. I had no idea that the conversation we had shared totally offended him—nor did I have a clue how angry he was. But I was about to find out.

Come the following business day, I got a clue as to just how offended Liam really was. I was notified that Liam wanted to file a grievance against me with my supervisor. I was blindsided and dumbfounded to say the least.

I'll be honest—my first impulse was to fight back. None of my co-workers had ever accused me of anything, let alone filed a grievance against me! I needed to calm down, because it would not be pretty if I let this get the better of me and destroy everything I held dear. There was much at stake: most importantly, God's glory.

I took a deep breath, and then I stated the obvious: "It's clear that Liam did not understand the intent of my heart. But you know what, there is nothing I can do if he wants to file a complaint. Let him go ahead and file. My entire team will stand with me. All the people I have dearly loved for all these many years will testify on my behalf."

She agreed and quickly said, "You know, after hearing your side of the story, and knowing your heart and history with our team, I think you're right. I think he totally misunderstood the intent of your heart. What do you say to taking Liam out to lunch and clearing the air?"

And that's exactly what we did. We took Liam to lunch and I am so glad we did. It was awkward, but so worth it.

Liam was extremely gracious, given his history with people of faith who had been less than kind to him. I was able to share real-life stories with Liam and talk about the relationship I shared with my staff and what they meant to me. Liam agreed that he had not understood the intent of my heart, and we moved from his being offended to a cautious acceptance of my offer of friendship.

A little more than a week or two after Liam and I had made our peace, I was working late one evening, alone in my office, when the phone rang. It was Liam—he was crying. He had been assaulted, severely beaten, and wanted to know if he could come to my office and speak with me.

I'll be honest, I was a little hesitant—nope, I was a lot hesitant. I was glad we had reconciled and that everything was okay between us, but I never wanted to experience that again. I didn't know if I was willing to put my heart on the line for Liam and risk being misunderstood or face another filed grievance. This was a moment to love even when that love had been severely tested. I got it. I understood what was a stake. So, I told him, "Come on by, Liam, I'll be waiting for you."

A little while later he knocked softly on my door. Trying to keep it light, I casually said, "Come on in, my friend." He slowly peeked around the doorframe. His handsome face was battered and bruised. I put my hand over my mouth, and blinked back tears. My heart was overwhelmed.

I don't know what possessed me, but I blurted, "Liam, tell me about your mom. Does she hug you very much?" He sniffled, "Sometimes—yeah, sometimes she does." I said, "Well, right now, I think you need a hug and I'd like to give you one, but I'm afraid you might file a complaint."

He started to weep and said, "Oh, Miss Joan, I could really use a hug right now." In that moment, I threw caution to the wind and just hugged the boy. He buried his head on my shoulder and let the tears fall. Oh, for grace to love more freely!

A few short weeks ago, Liam thought I was his enemy, and I thought he had it in for me. But God had other plans—plans for Liam to experience the Father's Love in a time of great need.

As our conversation drew to an end, I looked over at Liam and mustered up the courage for one final blessing. I smiled at him and with a twinkle in my eyes said, "Liam, if it's not too much, I would really like to pray for you . . . but then again, I'm still afraid that you might file a complaint."

He looked over at me and tears welled in his eyes, and then he said, "I could really use your prayers, and I promise—no complaint will be filed."

I reached across the desk, took his hands in mine, bowed my head, and prayed.

I prayed that God would mend his wounded body and heal his broken heart. I prayed that Liam would know how much the Father loved him, that his life would be full of joy, and that the blessings of God would fall upon him all the days of his life.

DISCUSSION (10 MINUTES)

Have you ever had a situation like Joan describes here where things seemed to go completely wrong? How did that feel? What did you do?

How should we deal with it when things go wrong or we are misunderstood?

How do you feel about Joan and Liam's reconciliation?

What are some opportunities you have to show love in small ways that end up being big gestures of God's love for people?

Debrief (10 minutes)

How can remembering the principle of A & B Relationships help direct our responses, even when we've been legitimately wronged by others?

What is something we talked about in this session that you hadn't thought about before or caused you to think about something differently?

What is something we talked about in this session that you could do differently starting tomorrow?

What else stood out to you in this session?

Closing & Prayer

Ask your group members what individuals have come to mind during this Bible study and how you can pray for them.

Session Six

WOMAN'S IMMEASURABLE WORTH

Welcome & Prayer (5 minutes)

Ask the Lord to open hearts and minds to His message and that each woman there would sense her immeasurable worth.

Content (5-10 minutes)

Play Session 6 Video 1 or read the "A Seat at the Table" passage below aloud (from pp. 52-60 of Made to Make a Difference).

A Seat at the Table

My second momma and I had made plans to attend a Christian women's luncheon where a wonderful Bible teacher that we both respected was to be the key note speaker. When we arrived at the venue, the room was filled to capacity and we could not find a place to sit. We searched everywhere looking for a place to sit—but to no avail. It seemed as though every seat was taken.

In a last-minute sweep of the room, we spotted two openings at a table near the front. As we started to take a seat at the table, we were quickly apprehended and told in no uncertain terms that we could not sit there because the guest speaker would be sitting at that table. My sweet momma said, "But we cannot find a seat anywhere." Regrettably, our dilemma fell on deaf ears because those "table police" couldn't have cared less.

As best as I can remember, no one offered to help us find a place to sit. In a room full of women wanting to walk with Jesus, not one person came forward to say, "Please join us; we'd love to have you sit at our table."

I know it may seem like a little thing, but it's not, not really. Because instead of being able to recall the beautiful moments of that gathering and the nuggets of truth that impacted our lives, I can't recall a single word that speaker said. Yet decades later, I can remember exactly how it felt to be told we were not welcome to sit at the speaker's table regardless of the fact that we could not find a place to sit anywhere else.

I couldn't help but wonder, "My goodness, have these women never read James, Chapter two, verse one? 'My dear brothers and sisters, how can you claim to have faith in our glorious Lord Jesus Christ if you favor some people over others?'" I'm just saying--it was pretty obvious that unless you were somebody special, part of the favored few, you were not welcomed to sit at that table.

The truth of the matter is that it is a sad state of affairs when we think more highly of ourselves than we should—when we exclude others because they are not part of "our circle." Thankfully, not everyone misses the opportunity to invite a stranger to share a seat at their table.

A few years ago, I had an opportunity to hear Angela Yuan share one of the most impactful testimonies I have heard in all my life.

She had decided life was just too painful. Her husband didn't love her, and her children no longer needed her. So, she made the decision to end her life. With nothing but her purse, she boarded a train to see her youngest son one last time—before taking her life. But on that ride, she happened to read a little pamphlet that had been given to her—a pamphlet that told her how precious she was to God and that He loved her and sent His only son that she might come to know His love for her.

She had never heard the gospel—she grew up in an atheistic home. She said she met Jesus on that train, and everything changed. For the first time in her life she had a sense of belonging and knew she was loved. In a short period of time, she led her husband and her oldest son to the Lord.

But the youngest son, the one she had gone to see one last time before leaving this world, was in a heap of mess. He ended up in prison—with a 20-year sentence.

But that didn't faze that momma. She had found Jesus and just like God had never given up on her, she wasn't about to give up on her son. For the next seven years, every single day, she spent hours praying for that boy. And every Monday, she fasted for that boy—for seven years! And just as she believed, there came a day that her boy found Jesus —like for real.

One day, while still in prison, he told his momma, "Do you think you can send me some information and an application from that Bible school in Chicago called Moody Bible Institute?" Well, that momma was so surprised she about dropped the phone in the kitchen sink.

Would they let an ex-convict, a guy with prison record, into that school? She could pray about it. And the answer to her prayer is nothing short of miraculous. In fact, it's kind of mind-blowing, but isn't that just like our God? He loves to answer bold prayers.

Shortly after her son had shared his dream of attending Moody Bible Institute, she and her husband attended a conference in Dallas. The first night they sat near the back of the room straining to hear the speakers. The next morning her husband got up early and went to the banquet room. He put their Bibles down on a table near the front. After breakfast they worked their way to the front of the packed room.

She said, "We'd only been seated a moment when Leon and I looked at each other, both feeling that something wasn't quite right. I glanced at the name tag of the woman next to me. Marge Malwitz, it read. I know that name from somewhere, I thought."

It didn't take long to realize that they had accidentally reserved their seats at the speakers table. They tried to apologetically escape. But Mrs. Malwitz put her hand on one of their Bibles and insisted that they stay. She introduced herself, her husband, and that morning's speaker: the president of Moody Bible Institute.

Now this momma knew that while she and her husband were surprised to be at the head table, this was no accident. God put them in that place at that time for a particular reason. She spent the entire time Dr. Joseph M. Stowell was speaking praying for the words to say.

When he sat back down at the table this is how it came out:

> "I stammered, "Dr. Stowell... I... I have a quick question..." "Yes"—he looked at my name tag—"Mrs. Yuan?"
>
> "Dr. Stowell," I asked, "does... does Moody accept sinners?"
>
> Dr. Stowell paused and gave me a perplexed look.
>
> "Well," I continued, "the reason why I ask is because my son will be coming out of prison soon. And he wants to study at Moody." I explained a bit more about Christopher's past and his current situation.
>
> Dr. Stowell thought for a moment, then asked me a simple but profound question. "Has he been redeemed?"
>
> A smile spread across my face, and I dropped my tense shoulders.
>
> "Yes," I said and sighed. "He has been. He has been redeemed."[1]

The people at that table, unlike the people at the other table I shared about earlier, welcomed two strangers to dine with them. And the rest is history because that momma's boy not only had his prison sentence miraculously shortened to three years, he graduated from Moody Bible Institute in 2005, received a Master of Arts in Biblical Exegesis from Wheaton College in 2007, and Doctor of Ministry from Bethel Seminary in 2014.

So, this is what I want to leave with you: There may be moments when you are deeply wounded—when you are not invited to have a seat at the table. I will not pretend that it does not hurt, because it does. And while it is true, that in the body of Christ there is no room or reason to ever marginalize anyone, it happens. We live in a fallen world and we are not yet perfected. Unfortunately, every one of us still stumble, still fall, and, at times, still hurt others. I wish this were not true, but it is.

Just like Isaac had to dig another well and then another well, until there was room enough for Isaac to flourish in all of life, may you find the courage to set your own table and then throw a party. Invite others to a seat at your table and let them know they are loved, they are wanted, and they matter deeply in the kingdom of God. Because this is what I know: God will not waste your pain.

He will take that pain (if you give it to Him) and turn it into your greatest potential, your greatest ministry, your greatest opportunity. That is what God does when we trust Him with all the things that have shattered our dreams and broken our hearts. He is the redeemer of all things.

. . .

Discussion (10-15 minutes)

Have you ever felt like Joan and her spiritual momma, like you didn't have a seat at the table or weren't worthy of one? What happened? What were some of the emotions you experienced?

Have you ever felt like Angela Yuan and were ready to give up? How did you pull out of it?

What did you think of the end of Angela's story?

What is something a little bit scary you could do like Angela did that might make a huge impact for someone else or even yourself?

Full Study Debrief (20 minutes)

What are some of the things you experienced in this study? What was the most difficult? What was the most enjoyable?

How do you feel about this Sacred Work in Secular Places study?

What did you like the most? And why?

What do you wish had gone differently and why?

If you had to explain what the major takeaways of this study, what would you say?

What stood out the most to you and why?

Closing & Prayer

Ask how you can specifically pray for each of your group members and pray aloud for them by name.

_____

_____

_____

_____

_____

_____

_____

_____

_____

_____

_____

_____

_____

Next Steps

Congratulations! You should be proud of yourself for courageously stepping out to lead your small group.

We hope it was an incredible experience, not only for your group, but also for you as a (reluctant) leader.

Even though the final session marks the end of this study, it's the beginning of a rewarding journey. We're looking forward to the stories you may hear in the coming weeks—or even years from now— about how this time in fellowship has impacted the lives of your group members and the people God puts in their lives.

So, what's next? We hope you stay in touch with us. And, if you haven't already downloaded it, we'd love to have you check out *The Reluctant Leader's Guide to Asking Better Questions*.

This simple, free guide provides an overview of the approach we used in creating the study you just completed. Now that you have experience leading dynamic group conversations we want you to have this valuable tool to see how you can apply those skills to any future group study.

To download your copy of *The Reluctant Leader's Guide to Asking Better Questions* visit:

https://capshawmedia.groovepages.com/thereluctantleadersbetterdiscussions/

About the Authors

Joan L. Turley is an author, speaker and business coach specializing in helping individuals and organizations "turn work hours into joy hours."

Her award-nominated book, <u>Sacred Work in Secular Places</u>, chronicles her unexpected journey out of full-time ministry work and into the secular workforce—ultimately finding her own mission field in corporate culture. Using compassion gained through her own experience, Joan helps readers, clients, and audience members chart their own courses to overcome insecurities and embrace the opportunities God puts in their paths.

She is an encourager with a capital E!

While serving for almost a decade as the director of operations for a prestigious salon and day spa in Houston, TX, she developed her signature shepherd-leadership skills. Nothing makes her happier than seeing people thrive through the work of their hands.

With a strong belief that God created work to be a blessing and not a curse, Joan became a certified John Maxwell Leadership Coach and Deeper Path Coach. A bold advocate for reversing ever-growing job dissatisfaction, Joan is teaching women how to go from the WORDplace in His Presence to the WORKplace in His Power.

When she's not busy working, Joan wants you to know that her favorite place is out on her front porch. She loves being out there drinking her strong-brewed Cafe du Monde and swapping stories with her snowy-white-headed man, her two grown children, and the one and only GRANDboy that she loves with all her heart. She's also very fond her two Australian Shepherds, Maybelle Rose and Harlan Tucker. She and her husband reside in Nashville, TN.

Connect with her at JoanLTurley.com or email her at Joan@JoanLTurley.com.

Marian L. Ward brings a unique background to the mix with experience in the academic and political arenas.

After spending about a decade consulting for political campaigns and non-profits, she shifted her focus back to school.

She holds a BA and an MA in communication and has taught communication courses at the college level for several years.

As time went on, the Lord placed a burden Marian's heart and opened opportunities for her to shift the sacred into the secular and she was able to start her own women's small group, the TRIBE for women from her church in her home. She could marry classroom facilitation skills to the more intimate setting and engage her skills in direct discipleship.

Additionally, Marian is working on a startup recovery ministry for women dealing with drug and alcohol addiction called At the Well Women's Restoration Ranch.

If you are interested in knowing more about that ministry, check out atthewellranch.org

Marian grew up on the Texas Gulf Coast in a little town called Santa Fe, about halfway between Houston and Galveston. After several years in the DC area and New Hampshire, she now lives near lots of extended family in Haskell, Arkansas, about a half hour south of Little Rock.

Marian wants you to know she loves Red Molly (her shelter mutt), coffee, Pittsburgh Steeler football, and her plethora of nieces and nephews. She has also become a prolific oil painter in the style of Bob Ross and is really enjoying making happy little trees and mountains.

Connect with her at MarianLWard.com or email her at Marian@MarianLWard.com.

Teri Capshaw is an author, blogger, wife, and home-schooling mom. Her award-winning book, *Dying to Win: How Inspire and Ignite Your Child's Love of Learning in a Overstressed World*, was inspired by her family's time spent in living abroad and realizing the immense pressure modern families are under in every corner of the globe.

Teri is passionate about helping women see their own worth, calling out greatness in their children, and building resilient families. More importantly she wants everyone to experience the peace and love available from knowing and joyfully accepting Jesus.

Teri has a wide range of interests, or, as her husband once explained to their kids, "Mommy does weird things." She enjoys researching, reading, and experimenting regularly on their homestead where they keep the world's strangest Jersey milk cow along with numerous more normal (thankfully) farm animals including chickens, ducks, turkeys, and, of course a horse, dog, and cat.

Teri is a former television journalist who grew up in the Black Hills of South Dakota. She was home-schooled K-12 (which was a really strange thing in the 1980s). She also has experience working in the political arena and served as the Donor Relations Officer at Campaign for Liberty from 2009 through 2013.

She left that position to spend several years living in Taiwan for her husband's job. In spite of the dedicated efforts of a tutor, she only learned enough Mandarin to order ice cream or milk tea and apologize when her kids did something weird in a public place. She blogs at tericapshaw.com and homesteadlarder.com.

Teri and her husband, Jesse, have five young children and live near Sand Hollow, Idaho.

Acknowledgments

A note from Joan...

I would like to thank my life-long friend, founder of Crossroads In Life Coaching, Christiana Martin, for encouraging me to stay the course. You spoke life over me when I felt like giving up.

I also want to thank Ronnie Mitchell, Senior Pastor of New Livingstone Church and Nashville City Network Leader with Made to Flourish. When I despaired that maybe, just maybe, I had misunderstood His calling, you affirmed His work in my life, as only a pastor can do. Thank you for listening and for believing in me.

And to my precious son, Nathan Turley, for always being willing to spend countless hours doing amazing graphic design work. This cover looks amazing! And to my husband, Ken Turley, your unwavering belief in my life's work is the rock beneath my feet. No one loves me better than you.

Lastly, Teri and Marian, time spent with the two of you is one of God's greatest gifts to me. I love ya to the moon and back!

A NOTE FROM MARIAN...

I would first like to thank my TRIBE at Celebration Baptist Church. These ladies were so patient with the process of building this study and provided invaluable feedback for this project. So, to Andreina, Charissa, Courtney, De'Lana, Jamie, Janet B., Janet H., Jodi, Laura, Marj (my mom of almost 40 years), Nancy, Robin, and Stephanie (my best friend for almost 30 years) ... thank you from the bottom of my heart.

I'd also like to thank my pastor, Allan Eakin, for believing in me and giving me freedom to work in my strengths in ministry.

And last but not least, my writing team partners, Joan and Teri. We are sisters now and I love you like crazy. Your support and encouragement has meant the world to me and I look forward to more fun and innovative projects with you.

A NOTE FROM TERI...

I want to thank my husband, Jesse. You are my dependable cheerleader every step of the way and I love you more than words can say. I'd also like to thank my precious children. Eliana, David, and Jonathan you helped make most lunchtime meetings a little quieter than would have been possible otherwise. You inspire me with every idea and question. Claire and Justin, you provided the smiles we all need.

I also want to thank Joan and Marian for including me in this project—you are the best friends any woman could ask for. I love you and look forward to the future as we grow together.

Notes

Session One

1. Theology of Work, The Bible and Your Work Study Series:
   Women and Work in the Old Testament, Peabody, Massachusetts: Hendrickson Publishers Marketing, LLC, 2015), 10
2. https://truthspeaker.wordpress.com/2011/02/03/david-and-svea-flood/, printed April 5, 2019

Session Two

1. Sherman, Robert B. and Sherman, Richard M. *Mary Poppins*. DVD. Directed by Robert Stevenson. Walt Disney Studios, 1964.

Session Three

1. Matte, Gregg. "More Than a Paycheck." Sermon, Houston's First Baptist Church, Houston, TX.
2. Cairney, Trevor, "Don't Waste Your Life at Work," *The Gospel Coalition Australia*, May 15, 2015, https://australia.thegospelcoalition.org/article/dont-waste-your-life-at-work (Quotes Justin Taylor)
3. Keller, Timothy with Katherine Leary Alsdorf, *Every Good Endeavor*, (New York: Riverhead Books, 2012), 54-55.
4. Keller, Timothy with Katherine Leary Alsdorf, *Every Good Endeavor*, (New York: Riverhead Books, 2012), 225.
5. Keller, Timothy with Katherine Leary Alsdorf, *Every Good Endeavor*, (New York: Riverhead Books, 2012), 227.

6. Russell, Mark L., and Gibbons, Dave, *Our Souls At Work*, (Boise, ID: Russel Media), 52, 53.

Session Six

1. Christopher Yuan, Angela Yuan, Out of A Far Country, (Colorado Springs, Colorado: WaterBrook Press, 2011)

www.ingramcontent.com/pod-product-compliance
Lightning Source LLC
Chambersburg PA
CBHW022341280326
41934CB00006B/726